PEACH TREE SWITCHES

No discipline is enjoyable while it is happening—it's painful!

But afterward there will be a peaceful harvest of right

living for those who are trained in this way.
Hebrews 12:11

By

Wondrous McHenry-Roach

FOREWORD

After a phone conference with my siblings a few years ago, we agreed on the necessity of sharing what life was like during our formative years. *Peach Tree Switches* was originally written only for my family. However, sharing these stories with my students during my years in education let me see their hunger for history. I hope they, and future generations, will appreciate the lessons learned as much as I enjoyed sharing. These are snippets from my perspective of home life and life in the community where I lived from the early 1950's to the early 1970's in South Arkansas.

These were the days before home phones, cell phones, Face Book, etc., and not long before those big microwave ovens. Things shared in this account reflect my attitude about several areas of my early years of life. Namely: my family's love, reverent fear of God, growing pains, inequality, and the results of discipline dispensed by my daddy with peach tree switches. It also explains why there are no more peach trees at our family's home place. William Earl and I, along with our siblings older than us, played a large part in causing the destruction of the trees. Only Gary, the youngest, was wise enough to conserve, but it was too late.

My view of the world, during my foundational years, was like looking through "Rose colored glasses." This writing has allowed me to appreciate the value of a stable family life. Were we perfect? Absolutely not! Did we love each other? Absolutely! I hope this kind of family love continues in future generations of our family and in others. Maya Angelou once said, ***"I've learned that people will forget what you said, people will forget what you did, but people will never forget how you made them feel."*** When I think of home, I feel safe.

IN REMEMBRANCE OF

LOUIE AND EVELYN MCHENRY

AND DEDICATED

TO THEIR DECENDANTS!

TABLE OF CONTENTS

1. HOME 1

2. EARLY LESSONS 8

3. THE DOWN–UP—DOWN—UP YEAR.......................21

4. BECOMING SOCIAL/STILL LEARNING...................26

5. HIGH SCHOOL..29

6. DARK DAYS..36

7. MORE DARKNESS 43

8. LIFE CONTINUES..45

9. LOOKING TO THE FUTURE..................................48

10. SIBLING EXTRAS 53

11. STORY NOTES...55

1. HOME

"There is nothing like family!" Words I have heard and read many times. The older I get, the more my mind takes mini vacations back to my childhood when I thought that no family could have as good of a time together as mine! I am Louie and Evelyn McHenry's youngest daughter, born on September 18, 1952, and given a very unusual name by my paternal grandmother, Wondrous. Being the skinny, youngest daughter of ten children with only one younger brother, you would think I was spoiled and got away with whatever I did. NOT! My parents believed the Bible verse that said, "Train up a child (male or female) in the way he should go and when he is old, he will not depart from it." That meant a trip to our small grove of peach trees at certain times for my siblings and me.

I have many fond memories of our home. To me, everything and everyone was beautiful. The sky, trees, grass, and believe it or not, sand. We did not have grass in our front yard when I was growing up. There were flowers, but they were in the flower bed bordering our house. There were cats, dogs, hogs, cows, and, at one time, chickens, and a horse! (Or it might have been a mule; it was used in plowing our vegetable garden). There was plenty of room for all on our two acres of land. It was always an exciting time when a cow got out of our cow pen. We couldn't let our source of milk, buttermilk, butter, and future beef get away. The two cows I remember were "Red" and "Blackie." Daddy would kill a calf every year, so we had plenty of steaks and roasts. He would also kill a hog every year. That was our bacon, sausage, ham, etc. I never ate the delicacy called chitterlings; nor did I try daddy's delicacy on hog killing day: hog brains scrambled with eggs- NOT for me! We learned about sharing by watching our neighbors help my dad, and in return, they got a share of the meat to carry home for their families.

Back then, the nights in the country were very dark, but we were not afraid. On hot summer nights, if we asked, we might have been allowed to sleep on the front porch. The night sounds through the open windows would lull us to sleep along with the sound of music on our radio. One type of bird would sing its name during the summer months, "Bob White;" at least that's how Mama explained it to me. Sitting on the front porch with her was so peaceful. Daddy and my brothers would be watching television. There was only one in our house, but we would talk and watch the sky. That is how I learned, *Star light, star bright, first star I see tonight. Wish I may, wish I might, have the wish I wish tonight.* Also, I learned, *I see the moon; the moon sees me. God bless the moon; God bless me.*

Daddy worked in the Bag Pack division of the International Paper Company in Cullendale, a community just outside of Camden. In my eyes, he was the best in everything he did. He provided well for his family, and my mother never had to work outside of our home. They were a team, and we never questioned their love. Days at our house meant getting up around five o'clock every day, weekends, too. My older siblings were already or almost out of the house in my memories. I slept in the room with my parents on a twin-size bed; they slept in a full-size bed. My four brothers still at home doubled up in two full-sized beds across the hall. Our parents insisted that we eat breakfast together at the table before Daddy would leave for work. When breakfast was ready, mama would call for us. I would get up immediately. However, my brothers needed a little extra motivation occasionally. If they moved too slowly in daddy's opinion, with a switch in hand, he would pull back their quilts and apply heat. Daddy had a ready source of switches with all the peach trees adjacent to our house. Like others who lived in the beautiful suburbs of Camden, near Louann, Arkansas, our veggies and fruits were homegrown. The potatoes, tomatoes, purple hull peas, watermelons, turnip greens, cabbage, and corn provided homework for my parents and my brothers with plowing, planting, weeding, and whatever else they did when we weren't in or after school. We had gardens on both sides of our house. The fertile ground around the peach trees was where cabbages, turnips, onions, peppers, etc. were grown, but the peach trees were my favorite and my scariest. A fresh peach, peach jelly, peach preserves, peach cobbler ... Oh yes, but those same trees produced some of the best switches parents could find for discipline.

My infractions showed I needed an attitude adjustment from time to time. Rolling my eyes at my mother when I didn't want to do something or hitting my brother William Earl (as we called him/ child number eight) when he annoyed me were my weaknesses. You would think that at some point I would have learned my lesson, but no, not me. I recall one Christmas morning I got an archery set (rubber-tipped arrows) and William got a toy pistol and holster that he could belt around his waist. It was decorated in a fancy way with silver metal parts. He started a fight with me (That's my story, and I'm sticking to it), and I hit him on the head with the holster. It made a lump rise on his forehead.

Daddy didn't say anything, but we knew. When he got up from where he sat, he headed to the peach trees—a whooping for both of us. Sometimes we'd try to change his mind by talking nicer to each other and complimenting him when we knew what was about to happen. NOT! I got my last "whooping" at home when I was seventeen and a senior in high school from my father on a Sunday morning. I was told to wash the dishes after breakfast. There went my rolling eyes, and there went my dad to the peach trees.

Although my daddy was the disciplinarian and did most of the whooping, [1] he did have a tender heart toward his family and community. I recall one night when the Miss America Pageant was on tv. The host started to sing the theme song, and I put a big towel around myself for a cape and a pillowcase over my head like long hair. My daddy sang, "There she is, Miss Louann." He also provided transportation when necessary for those in need in our community.

My earliest memory was when I was four years old. Having a lot of children in our house every day would have been too much. God knew that, so the first set of children, ranging in age from twenty-three to seventeen, were on their way out: college, military, marriage, and graduation. One of that first set, Georgia Marilyn, had passed away as a five-week-old baby before I was born. She had jaundice, but in 1939, my parents didn't know the cure was simply exposing her to sunlight for a few hours a day. I remember being told my mother had a nervous breakdown after her baby died. It started before my time, but I think that was when getting her out of the house became a necessity: going for a ride, going to a drive-in movie, going to visit family…all helped her deal with the loss and kept her mind focused.

Another early memory was when most of the family was in the den one night talking. No one was paying me any attention even in my blue and white polka dotted dress with fancy ruffled panties underneath. I was used to getting attention. I demanded attention. I wanted attention! So, I politely got up, walked to the door, bent over, and patted myself

4

on the behind to them all. Daddy got up! I had gotten his attention. He didn't talk to me or explain anything. I tried to run to other family members, but nobody saved me. The message was swift, clear, and painful. I never did that again. Bad behavior checked for the moment! Thank you, daddy!

The one and only time my mother whooped me came after she and I walked to the house of one of our adult cousins who lived a quarter of a mile from us. Mama had told me not to "show out." I don't remember what I did, but it came under the category of "showing out." At least she waited until we got back home to give me some attention. She did a very good job. Lesson learned. Thank you, mama!

Our house was right across the small dirt road from our church, Good Home Baptist Church. I could go inside the church whenever I wanted, and I wanted. I would do little clean -up jobs and play the piano. I started taking piano lessons when I was seven. I remember both sets of my grandparents paid for my lessons to help my parents out. Our family was blessed to have both sets of grandparents and our maternal great grandma, we called her "Mom Paralee," for many years. Grandma

Georgia and Grandpa Marshall McHenry were our paternal grandparents. Grandma Dolly and Grandpa Lee Gaskin were our maternal grandparents. All shared their love in whatever ways they could.

I remember how Grandpa Marshall would bring Grandma Georgia to the Mission meetings on Monday afternoons for the ladies in the church. He usually sat in the car and read the newspaper while he waited. I suppose I was still feeling the need for attention on one of those days. I sat in the car with him and started probing in his glove compartment. He still didn't pay me any attention until I pulled out his real pistol. I didn't know the danger in my hand, but he did. Newspaper quickly tossed aside, his voice became very gentle and very high pitched, "Baby, baby, give me that. Baby." I had his undivided attention then.

LESSON LEARNED: LOCK IT UP!

I enjoyed piano lessons with my first teacher. She served me my first scrambled egg sandwich! I did okay with the lessons, but piano really was just a hobby for me. My next piano teacher gave lessons at Good Home. Eventually, daddy bought a piano for me, and we would sit together while I would practice, and he sang. I loved it. I thought I was being smart with my next piano teacher. Lessons were at home, and he usually showed up around dinner time and ate with us. I'm sure he tried, but I was not as interested as my cousins who took lessons also. They excelled! Still, I am grateful for the lessons learned since I used my ability as an adult at our church and for my own entertainment.

When church services were big like Pastor & Wife's Anniversary, Singing Unions, funerals, etc., people would park their cars in our yard outside our fence. We did not mind. I could walk to church and walk home. I don't know why I never just left service and went home. At our house, the doors were never locked, and I don't remember being told not to leave. I think those peach trees did something to me. My awareness of right from wrong was activated. My piano playing now is mostly by ear and not by reading music. It still brings me joy during my meditation times.

I was confident and bold as a little girl. Daddy was a deacon and the Sunday School Superintendent at our church. At the end of the lesson study, he would give a review while walking from one side of the church to the other across the front of the sanctuary. Guess who would get up and walk beside him holding onto his leg and feeling very important... me. Proud of my daddy!

2. EARLY LESSONS

I remember being allowed to visit Lafayette; that was an African American school my siblings attended. I went with my sweet cousin, Lenora, before I started school. Of course, this was long before integration. I think she was in the sixth grade, and I was only about five years old. I had to stay with her all day at school. Her teacher was Mr. Lawson, and he permitted me to sit at the same big desk with her during class. To me the classroom looked enormous. The students all looked big, and most importantly, Mr. Lawson WAS the authority in the classroom.

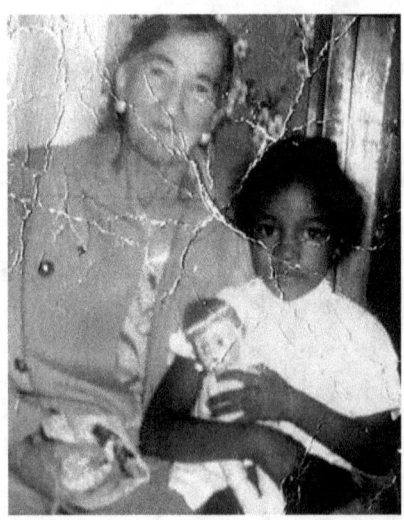

The floors must have been wooden because while he was lecturing, a boy fell asleep at his desk in class. That was a big "No No!" Mr. Lawson pulled out what to me looked like a horse whip and expertly cracked it on the wooden floor beside the boy's desk. That woke him up and anyone else with napping on their minds. That was the most memorable part of my day and the first classroom rule I learned...

NO SLEEPING IN CLASS!

When our oldest brother, HL – he gave himself the name Henry Lee when the military required more than initials- came home from the military, we were always so happy to see him. He treated William Earl, Gary (child number ten), and me like his little soldiers. He'd make us fall in line and march to his orders. He always treated me like he was my second daddy minus the peach tree switches.

Summers were so much fun. After doing what we were told, William Earl, Gary, and I would play outside all day. That meant freeze tag, jacks, hide and seek, or my favorite, "One-I-Catch!" One -I-Catch was our version of baseball. It only required three players: the pitcher, the batter, and the catcher. Many times, we improvised where the pitcher and catcher played dual roles and also became outfielders; more could play if available. The batter could toss the ball up and try to hit it. If you caught the hit ball on one bounce, (our balls bounced) you became the batter. If you were able to throw the ball from the field inside the extended bat and the bent-sideways batter, you became the batter. If the pitcher threw a strike and the catcher caught it on one or no bounce, he became the batter. The ground we played on was hard with no grass, so the bouncing part was easy. We had to make our own ball with masking tape and a lot of string. A good stick served as our bat, and we were ready! I only remember playing with my brothers. Being the only girl was no big deal. Sure, we fussed sometimes, but that was and is the way of siblings, especially William Earl and me.

If the weather was unfavorable, we played Scrabble or Sorry mostly inside. When we got a television, we did not keep it on all day long. TV was entertaining with options like: The Three Stooges, The Flintstones, Tarzan, The Real McCoys, The Beverly Hillbillies, etc. We were very happy when Julia began to air. In fact, whenever a Negro came on, it was so special. The alarm was sounded, "There's a Negro on tv!" was a rarity and always brought us together to watch.

My world was my family. Even when I started school, we had little rituals before we got on the bus. We would know about the time we had to be at the bus stop when we heard the school bus. One of us would break out in our own song, "Bus gone down the ro~~a~~d. " That meant the bus was passing by our stop and would be back around in about three minutes to get us.

We would gather our things, say goodbye to Mama, and head out. If it was a rainy day, we'd walk as far as our church and stand on the steps under the small covering until we heard the bus. Our driver was always Mr. Charles A. Yarbrough. Mama taught us to always say, "Good morning, Mr. Yarbrough," "Good evening," and "Bye" showing respect to Mr. Yarbrough. A lot of students called him "Charles A." I never did, and my siblings didn't either that I know of. I once heard Mr. Yarbrough make a remark about a boy who was being disrespectful toward him. After the boy got off the bus, Mr. Yarbrough mumbled, "Half-raised fool." I knew to be called a "fool" was a bad thing. Sometimes people will make you say things uncharacteristic of yourself. Frustrated, I'm sure, but Mr. Yarbrough always said "bye" after we said "Bye, Mr. Yarbrough" while getting off the bus. He even let us all have a little fun at times. There was a spot on our bus route home where those sitting on the back seats would start bouncing and would bounce high when Mr. Yarbrough hit the big bump that was in the gravel road. It was fun. I liked Mr. Yarbrough.

My early days of school were good if my classmates and I behaved ourselves. There was no kindergarten in 1958 in our school system. I started school with first grade. We had all grades on the same campus, first through twelfth. Mrs. McGhee was my first-grade teacher, and although she could be a little strict, I loved her, and I wanted to stay on her good side.

I recall during Christmas season in her classroom, someone sitting near the door of the classroom yelled out, "Santa Claus just walked by!" We all jumped out of our seats, jammed the doorway, and peeped out. Suddenly, I felt Mrs. McGhee's strap across my back. Uh oh! She struck quickly, and I believe no one at the door escaped a strap lick across the back. Life lesson learned…

GET PERMISSION BEFORE GETTING OUT OF YOUR SEAT!

I think Mrs. McGhee got sick or something later in the school year. I remember being told her niece, Ms. Dennis, would take her place. She did, and she was sweet, too. However, I still missed Mrs. McGhee.

On one day in first grade, a classmate told me she was going home with me. Sure enough, she got on my school bus and did just that. I suppose my parents made sure her parents knew where she was, but the thing I remember most is this—On the next day, mama dressed her in one of my dresses (girls didn't wear pants to school back then) and sent us to school. It was a red plaid dress and a favorite of mine that Mama had made herself. I never got that dress back.

Second grade was not as pleasant. I loved Mrs. Jones, my teacher, but there was a girl in my class who didn't like me. I never knew why. She told the other girls they couldn't play with me at recess. Imagine, a second-grade bully! My true friends and cousins were still nice to me, but they too were afraid of her. She was bigger than most of us, and no one wanted to be beaten up by her. I was alone a lot, so I did my work well and got good grades. Life lesson learned…

IGNORING A BULLY CAN WORK IN YOUR FAVOR!

A very good thing happened to me during this time. Our church had our annual revival during the late Summer. After the sermon one night, my brother, William Earl, took the pastor's hand when the altar call was made. I watched my brother, and I did too. The pastor asked him what he wanted. William Earl said, "I believe the Lord has pardoned me of my sins, and I want to be baptized." I was asked the same thing; so, I parroted my brother, "I believe the Lord has pardoned me of my sins, and I want to be baptized. " That was my FIRST baptism, at seven years old, but in the days after, I seemed to have a revelation that I would never be the same again. Of course, I was still a child, and my brother and I still fought at times, but my love and respectful fear of the Lord was heightened after being baptized. God was up to something in my life.

I still found myself alone at recess, and I still got the cold shoulder from a few of my classmates, but again, I ignored them and never tried to retaliate. I wasn't angry at anybody for the way I was treated. Down deep they weren't really friends with the bully. They were protecting themselves. To God be the glory! This was an ongoing life lesson I learned...

TROUBLE DON'T LAST ALWAYS, as the lyrics of the song say.

I do remember having a dream around this time of my life that has served to encourage me and give me hope all my life. In my dream, I looked out of a window of our house at the night sky and saw different shapes in the sky. The one that I remember most was that of a lamb. Then, the darkness disappeared to reveal a huge, creamy white mansion with several huge columns in front! The ground it set on looked like fluffy clouds. In my dream, a thought came to my mind: This is your heavenly home. All these years later, I am still excited about my mansion in heaven.

When our pastor at Good Home, Rev. Mullins, passed away, Rev. E. Bowie eventually was chosen to pastor our church. He came with his wife and daughter who both were "songbirds!" His daughter was older than me, and she treated me like her little sister. During those days, the pastor's family would eat at a church member's home after morning worship on Sundays. Since we lived just across the road, they ate with us often, I loved it. I enjoyed my "big sister" friend! She and I would lay across the bed in our guest bedroom with the curtains pulled open and the windows up in warm weather and talk, nap, or both. One time she invited me to come along with them to another member's home. I remember she must have invited others too because we all went walking in the woods. From where I don't know, someone pulled out a pack of cigarettes! We each got one and lit up. The coughing was too much for me. That was my first and last cigarette. I think I was around nine years old. Thank God we didn't start a fire in the woods! That would have been a guaranteed trip to the peach trees if my daddy had known.

My little brother, Gary, was at home with Mama all day while William Earl and I were at school. To give him a smile after school, I would bring a treat from the "store" (a private residence behind our school building). Daddy gave me a dime every day for school. With a nickel, I could buy a candy bar like Butternut, Hollywood, Big Time, or salted pretzels in a box. I could also get my favorite: two red cinnamon suckers for a nickel!!! Gary got a lot of suckers!

In third grade, I had Mrs. Nayles. I loved her, but the nonsense continued with another bully. I was dealing with two bullies! The newest one was the one who kept my red plaid dress in first grade! She would sometimes take my dime AND my food in the cafeteria. The other bully once took a saltshaker and shook salt all over my food in the cafeteria at lunch. I decided I'd had enough for that day. I faked a stomachache. The school secretary called my dad from work. Daddy came in, picked me up, carried me to his truck, and took me home to mama. Daddy was always my hero, and I was his baby girl. Home was my place of refuge.

It was in third grade that I first started to notice boys. Giggles meant a lot back then. A cute boy came to our class late in the school year, and most of us giggled a lot because we all had eyes for him. In third grade, he didn't seem to notice at all. In fact, none of the boys seemed to notice any of our giggles. Oh well, at least boys were a distraction from the antics of my bullies.

Mrs. Kennedy was my fourth-grade teacher. She was smart, pretty, and accepted no nonsense. I don't know why, but one day she had a few of us come to the front of the classroom and sing! A classmate and I sang, "*Soldier Boy*," by The Shirelles. That was fun and we did well.

Another time, our class did what we all did at Lafayette. We went to assembly in the gymnasium. As I remember, those assemblies began with a beautiful song for devotion with the words of Psalm 19:14, followed by singing The Lord's Prayer. Mrs. Kennedy had told us to sit up and pay attention at assemblies. I guess my friend and I thought that was a suggestion because once we got there, she and I started grooming each other's fingernails. When we got back to the classroom, we got called up to the front of the class again, but it wasn't to sing. I had not felt the strap since first grade, but I discovered it again with more power. Surprisingly, the strap had the same effect as daddy's switches! So it was, "Yes ma'am, Mrs. Kennedy." Lesson learned...

PAY ATTENTION IN ASSEMBLY!

It was in fourth grade that I learned a valuable life lesson. Class bullies were still active, and they still sought to disturb my peace, but reading became my outlet. I enjoyed the wealth of stories books offered me. When my classwork was finished, I would read. While others whispered among themselves, I read, and my mind went everywhere the stories led me. I loved it, and the bullies couldn't reach me. My true friends and I played at recess; we got chased by the cute boys in our class, and we got the "Do you like me? Circle yes or no" notes from the boys. We were all growing physically, academically, and socially. School was fun!

Next came the best grade of all my school years, FIFTH GRADE! At ten years old, I was too old to be thought of as a baby, but too young to be an obnoxious teenager. That was fine, but my fifth-grade teacher was amazing, Mrs. Mary Dunning!!! We had devotion in her classroom every morning. We would sing a patriotic song, say a scripture, and say the Lord's prayer.

On the days we sang, "God bless America," I soloed on a verse. *"While the storm clouds gather/far across the sea/ let us pledge allegiance / to a land that's free. Let us all be grateful for a land so fair/ as we raise our voices / in a solemn prayer ..."* then the famous chorus in unison. *"God bless America ..."*

Another thing that made that year great was my teacher's love for crafts! She could make useful items out of what some would consider junk. When William Earl, was in her class, he had brought home a beautiful table decoration made from two metal cans, two empty bathroom tissue rolls, and plaster of Paris painted and decorated, with beautiful plastic flowers sticking out through two holes (It was supposed to look like a log), I couldn't wait to be in fifth grade a couple of years later. One of our first projects was a purse made from popsicle sticks! Another time, we took fifteen wire clothes hangers, floral wire, spray paint, and artificial flowers and made hanging baskets! Mama put the one I made up in our dining area when I brought it home! It was pink and beautiful. I felt special!

It was also in fifth grade that my friend came to school one day wearing a beautiful pair of pink glasses. I asked her how she got to wear glasses. She told me she sat too close to the tv. I wanted glasses, too. So, I started sitting too close to the tv. Sure enough, at an eye exam, I was diagnosed as nearsighted. I had to wear glasses, too! What I didn't know was that her problem was corrected after a time, but I did quite a job on myself. My problem continues...

I was thrilled when Mrs. Dunning became my sixth-grade teacher, too! My taste for Vienna sausages began because of her. I didn't know about them until we saw her at lunchtime in the classroom. We'd see her eating when we got back from the school cafeteria: A small can of Vienna sausages, Ritz crackers, and a soft drink! Her lunch had a unique smell, but when I finally got to try them at home, I liked them, too.

LAFAYETTE
SCHOOL DAYS 1962-63

There were days in fifth and sixth that weren't so good–like the rainy day Mrs. Dunning told us not to go to the store (Ms. Lucille's store–I can't remember if the store closer to the school building was operational by this time) at recess because we'd have to walk across the muddy football practice field to get there.

We thought we were being smart, and all agreed that everyone in our class should go to the store because "Mrs. Dunning was too old to use her strap on the whole class." I suppose the mud on our shoes gave us away. After we came inside from recess, she had us all form a line.

My cousin said she was going to get hers over with first. Now, Mrs. Dunning didn't do the one, two, three, swat-and-go licks with her strap. It was more like Tyler Perry's Madea whooping where the whoopee

17

danced around the whooper. Seeing that, I decided to get at the end of the line, so she'd be tired by the time she got to me, but that "old lady" gave the same pain she'd given at the start to all of us. I was wearing a red velvet skirt, and when she was done with me, it had strap prints all over it from my dance around Mrs. Dunning. Lesson learned...

OBEY YOUR TEACHER!

Another thing I loved about Lafayette was what was called "Socials." Those had value in our community because they showed us how to behave in the company of the opposite sex. We learned how to respect each other in a social setting. If you paid a dime, you could attend this gathering in the gymnasium where popular music was played, and everyone danced and talked (socialized). If a boy didn't ask for a dance, some girls would dance together. I don't remember doing a lot of dancing at the socials, but they were socials, and we did enjoy being around other schoolmates. Proper distance between dance partners, proper hand position during slow dances, proper noise levels, acceptable dance moves, and proper language were monitored by teachers who were there and served as chaperones. I didn't realize that this was a learning experience then, but I understand now. Lesson learned...

PROPER ETIQUETTE!

Another place we could dance was at the same place my class had slipped off to, what I call "Con Lucille's." (Same as Ms. Lucille's and I'm not sure how we were cousins). At recess or lunchtime, her jukebox was always a draw for us music lovers. She also sold hot dogs, chips, big cookies, dill pickles, and soda pops. We could dine and dance, unchaperoned!

For little girls beginning to be more aware of themselves after getting into the double digits, little boys could be cruel. One classmate walked around the classroom one day when our teacher had stepped outside, announcing the pretty girls to the whole class. He would point to or lightly touch the ones he thought pretty. Although I was relieved to be named among the pretties, I empathized (I didn't know that word back then) with those he skipped over. Some dismissed him, but I'm sure there were hurt feelings. I have never enjoyed seeing anyone hurt or teased. I'm sure he meant no harm, but that didn't change the hurt for some.

At times, the teachers would need to send a message to another teacher by a student. One day, Mrs. Dunning had me take a note to my big brother's high school classroom. The students began to say how pretty I was when I walked in, and that endeared me to the class of 1964 forever. They made me feel like a little sister to each of them.

Another thing that was special about Lafayette was the special honor given to the twelfth-grade students. For one day during the school year, the seniors were given the opportunity to be a teacher for a day in the elementary classrooms. The seniors dressed and behaved like the adult authority in each classroom. We had to show respect and obey the student teachers as we would our regular teachers. It was a practice in humility for us all.

As a pesky little sister, I was always around when my brothers' friends came to play basketball in our backyard at home after school. My daddy wouldn't let me play sports at school because he thought the game was too rough for me. He didn't want to see his little girl get hurt. I did enjoy being around the big boys. Most of them were related somehow to us, but some were just cute guys.

3. THE DOWN–UP— DOWN—UP YEAR

The worst and best to happen during my sixth-grade school year happened in the Fall and Spring semesters respectively. On November 22, 1963, we stayed in school after lunch, but our teachers didn't teach. They were all distraught and sat in their classrooms with radios tuned to coverage of the assassination of President John F. Kennedy in Dallas, Texas. The whole school seemed to be covered in gloom. I think it was cloudy and cold that afternoon, or maybe it was the gloominess that covered our faces for the next few days.

When we got home, the sadness was there too as our older brothers and their wives joined us in watching the coverage on tv. I recall seeing HL's wife through a window walking up to the porch wearing sunglasses in no sunlight. I assumed it was to hide the redness in her eyes from crying. Mama babysat their daughter, my niece, Stephanie, for them while they both taught at Lincoln High School (the other African American school in Camden). I took comfort in helping and called Stephanie, "My baby!" She was just a toddler at the time of the assassination. "As soon as we get someone who cares about African Americans, [2] ... " We were angry and sad, but we didn't revolt. It felt like a death in everybody's family that Fall day. Seeing the funeral on tv a few days later added to the heaviness in our hearts. Empathizing and (that word again) and sympathizing with family and others were the right emotions back then, no matter your political views.

Although there were plenty then and there are some now, it is still hard to believe the coldness in some people's hearts. They remained unwilling to change even after hatred stirred up the devil in Dallas. I take comfort knowing God is Sovereign. After JFK's death, you could see artwork of his likeness in many African American homes. Even church hand fans were made with his picture on it keeping the people of God cool in the months ahead. His motto resonated in the hearts of many people, "Ask not what your country can do for you; ask what you can do for your country." Like us all, he had his faults, but to most like me, he was a decent man. Someone wrote in a song, "The good die young." He was only 46 years old.

Spring semester of sixth grade became my best time ever at school. The sixth grade students performed what was called an operetta! Our teachers judged auditions for parts, I think. I never auditioned. The title of the operetta was "Cinderella." Mrs. Dunning told me I was Cinderella! Wow! I had no choice in the matter. I still remember part of the song I had to sing and some of the other songs too. My mother made my ball gown out of yellow taffeta! My slippers were gold (white shoes spray-painted gold). All went well for me until the night of the show. There was a scene where Prince Charming (The same boy who had announced me among the pretties) sang to me, helped me stand and was supposed to kiss my hand. When he reached for it, I whispered, "You better not kiss my hand." He was smart. He bent over and kissed the air beside my hand. To this day, I don't know what was on my mind. Maybe I acted that way because my real Prince Charming, my daddy, was watching in the audience.

During that school year, there was more sadness. Have you ever noticed that many African American schools were built very near railroad tracks? One morning, our band director and his three children were almost at school when they were hit by the train that ran past our campus every day. At that time, there were no flashing lights or warning signals there, only the sign for railroad crossing.

It was touch and go all day as everyone waited for news of their conditions. To God be the glory that no one was killed, but I do believe there were long term health issues that resulted for them. The Bible says, "In all things, give thanks." We knew it could have been so much worse. The band director was my math teacher the following year when I was in seventh grade, and he was a great pianist. His son played the trumpet in the school's band and was my classmate, his oldest daughter was a talented singer (she sang at my wedding years later), and the younger daughter was one I considered as my little friend. Looking back, I can still remember how rumors kept spreading all day about the wreck. God's hand of protection had to be on them. Again, thank you, Lord!

The Summer before my seventh-grade school year (another mini-vacation moment in my mind) found part of our family traveling by car from Camden, Arkansas, to Fresno, California! Back then, that was the safest and least expensive way for the six of us. HL (oldest brother) and Alvernon (second born brother) took turns driving and sleeping. Traveling in those days called for planning and preparation. Daddy, Mama, Gary (youngest sibling), and I helped keep the driver alert and witnessed first-hand the beautiful scenery along the route. If memory serves me correctly, it took us almost three days to get there with only small rest stops along the highways.

Those were the days of "White Only" signs on restaurants, hotels, etc. I guess the idea of chicken in a shoe box was a good one. I don't remember what food we ate, but I do remember it wasn't much and it was what we brought with us mostly. There was a drive through window at one restaurant we stopped at near the end of our trip. We were told to place our order and drive around to the back to pick it up. Such were the sixties. Great days – NOT!

Relieving ourselves was another story. We could not stop at service stations along the route due to those pesky "White Only" signs. I recall that the route took us near a lot of railroad tracks. Our best solution was to stop on the side of the road near the tracks where they were somewhat elevated, walk over to the other side that was out of the view of traffic, and relieve ourselves. Gary was only six or seven years old, and an empty soft drink bottle was enough for his "Number one" relief when we couldn't stop very long.

When we finally made it, we stayed at my big sister, Melvia's house. She and her husband had four children with the oldest one Gary's age. I found myself too old to play with the other children but too young to be in adult conversations. I was also at that awkward time in my body. Nothing really fit, skinny, big glasses, unruly hair Oh well, I was in California for the first time!!!

I remember going to the beach with my cousin when we visited San Francisco. There were amusements there that were fun, but one stuck with me more than the others—the Scary House amusement ride at the beach! For about ten seconds into the ride, I was fine moving through the darkness at the beginning, but when I saw a "skeleton" jump out at us, I used my God given defense mechanism: I closed my eyes! I heard screams from my cousin and the other riders, but I didn't open my eyes until I sensed daylight, and the ride was over.

NO MORE SCARY RIDES FOR ME!

I don't recall how, but I earned a prize playing some game. I was allowed to choose it from a variety of prizes. I chose a beautiful blue Cross that my daddy brought back home and mounted on the pulpit at our church. It hung there for years. I even have a picture of our pastor, Rev. Bowie, standing in the pulpit behind it at my home church.

Before we left the beach that day, Gary and I got a little too close to the water for my daddy's comfort. We had taken off running toward the Pacific Ocean not knowing the danger of the loud, high waves. When I looked back, I saw daddy frantically yelling and beckoning us to come back. Like God protects us from dangers seen and unseen, our Heavenly Father and my earthly hero were watching over us.

4. BECOMING SOCIAL/STILL LEARNING

As a preteen, I still loved the Lord and going to church but for an added reason...boys! Those Singing Union services were the best because we would travel once a month on every third Sunday afternoon among five churches. Daddy was President of the Singing Union that met once a month at different churches and President of the Singing Convention that also traveled among more churches on every fifth Sunday afternoon of the year. At offering times, the youth would usually pay their offerings and keep walking outside to talk and visit until service was dismissed. I wanted to too, but daddy always told me to stay inside until service was over. I was not about to disobey him–possible peach tree consequences. I still managed to meet a few boys and socialize.

My brother, Carthell, who was six years older than me, liked the pretty, hired church pianist for Good Home as teenagers. My dad would take her home after church, and my brother and I would ride too. She had a brother a little older than my little fast self. Once, he held my hand during the ride home! I thought I was in love.

Not all relationships were about being boy crazy. I can't say that I even remember the classmate I have always considered *my brother from another mother*, and to him: *his sister from another mister* until we ended up in the same seventh grade classroom. In just clowning around one day, he held up my arm and turned me around several times showing he could because I was so little. He made me laugh, and our relationship has always been like siblings. This same "brother" and I still communicate from time to time to check on each other's family and health.

By eighth grade, my last year at Lafayette, the bullies were acting better! School was fun but a blur for me of playing the clarinet in the band, going on band trips, band practice, etc. I did okay in the band on my clarinet, but band was not a priority for me. A certain boy from Lincoln began to send messages to me after I met him on our school campus. For the next few years, we would see each other at sporting events, school socials, or church functions. I thought he was cool.

At the end of a school day, when I was in eighth grade, our literature teacher talked maybe a minute after the bell rang to end class and the school day. I walked out to go to the bus lot, but I noticed my three "cousin friends" were taking their time talking at the school lockers.   I turned around and told them they were going to miss the bus. We all walked together and got to the bus lot just in time to see the bus pull away.

There was only one thing I could do, call my daddy. I think the secretary had to call mama first, and mama must have called daddy at work. (It was a long- distance -call in that day and was a charge on our phone bill).

Daddy picked up all four of us in our family car. He usually rode in his truck to work, but he somehow had gotten our car to transport us girls. We rode home happily talking about how it was Mrs. Sterling's fault we had missed the bus. Daddy didn't say a word. I said goodbye to each one as daddy dropped them off at their houses. When we got home, I got out of the car and walked into the house. Daddy got out of the car and walked to the peach trees. With my heart beating fast and him making my little legs sting, he said, "Don't you ever talk about your teacher!" Lesson learned…

RESPECT YOUR TEACHER AT ALL TIMES.

I never missed the school bus again! Eighth grade was my last year at Lafayette. I remember Mr. Tyree Williams trying to prepare us for integration as best he could. He told us that when we got to Fairview, the white students were going to be more advanced than we were. I suppose that was because they always had gotten the newest textbooks when they came out. We had always gotten the ones they had used before getting the new ones. Back then, we had to write our names in our books. Mine was never the first name in my textbook. A list of white students' names filled each line where we were to put our names. That was just the way it was. The textbooks we got were worn, written in, and never with that new book feel and smell.

Because we had been taught at home, at church, and at Lafayette, we knew how to behave before going to Fairview. I didn't know that I would be one of the group that went to Fairview at that time. I didn't roll my eyes or dare question that decision. Lesson learned:

THE DECISION WAS NOT EASY FOR ANYONE.

5. HIGH SCHOOL

I made it to ninth grade around Fall of 1966, and my world was a maze of newness. "Freedom of Choice" was an option for African American students whose parents allowed them to attend the previously all white (Caucasian) school, Fairview. Many people realized integration was coming and wanted to "Test the waters." My dad was president of the PTA (Parent-teacher association) at Lafayette. He gave my older brother, William Earl, who was a junior, the option of staying at Lafayette or going to Fairview. He chose to integrate. My younger brother was in fourth grade, and it was no problem for him. Daddy didn't give me an option. He said go, and I went.

My older brother, Carthell, who had graduated from Lafayette High School in 1964, took me to Fairview High School on my first day. He had bought me a beautiful blue, denim dress with a colorful little scarf in front. For these new times, I remember a saying I used every day in getting ready for school, "Then was then; now is now." THEN was going to school with people who looked like me, shared the same love for music, had the same features as I did, and whose parents expected best behavior.   At Fairview, NOW was where some pronounced "Negro," "Niggre. " THEN, we had learned to show respect; Lafayette's teachers didn't stand for foolishness or mediocrity.   Our education seemed important to them. NOW meant getting on the Lafayette bus, being dropped off at French Port[3] boarding the Fairview bus that was full of white people. THEN, white people were an oddity to me. I had little to no contact with them other than seeing them on TV.   NOW, seeing them up front and personal, I noticed imperfections. The makeup was especially strange to me. The girls had pink faces and white necks.

One of the first lessons I learned was that Mr. Williams was wrong in his assessment of the advanced intelligence and honesty of the students at Fairview. The first time I took a test in class and saw a classmate cheat I recognized that the color of your skin is not a factor in what a person will or will not do. Lesson learned...

"PEOPLE ARE PEOPLE."

Many, but thankfully not all, of the boys and girls were full of mean looks and mean stares. If their goal was to make me feel uncomfortable, they succeeded. Walking in the hall meant being obviously avoided as if bumping or touching me would rub my color off on them.

There were times their avoidance was not so bad. William Earl played football for Fairview. If the bleachers were full, all we needed was an opening. Just find a space in the bleachers and sit. Then, all the whites around us would scatter allowing us comfortable seating. Again, not all the whites acted this silly, but quite a few did.

My ninth through twelfth grade years were unstable emotionally for me. I remember the first day I walked into a classroom at Fairview. It was my science classroom. I was the first one to get there, so I sat at a desk. Two white boys entered, saw me, and one said, "Man, we gotta get the KKK (I will not dignify this hate group with an explanation) down here. " The other boy laughed, but it was not funny to me. I had heard the evils of that detestable group. This was 1966, during the Civil Rights Movement. Dr. Martin Luther King, Jr. was still alive and actively working for our rights as American citizens. Headlines and newscasts reported killings and protests all the time as my race struggled for equal rights. On top of those feelings, the war in Viet Nam was hot, Politicians like George Wallace, Strom Thurman, and many others again kept the devil stirred up in the minds of people who refused to even try to understand that their thinking was hurtful and flawed. Sort of like our times...Who am I kidding? Like today!!!

It was in that same ninth grade science classroom that I got another rude awakening. There was only one girl besides me in a classroom full of white boys, mostly athletes, with a white football coach as the male science teacher. The white girl and I sat in a row near the windows with me at the front and her behind me. We learned to converse with each other cordially. I never witnessed any signs of toleration or empathy (that word again) from the teacher/coach toward us. We were just a couple of out of place females in his class. His football players appeared to be all he cared about, and they were the focus of his attention.

One day, the teacher/coach asked a question about our lesson and none of the boys even tried to answer. Their silence seemed to make him angry. I don't know why, but I raised my hand, got a frown filled nod from him, and I answered the question correctly. His face turned red, he pounded his fist hard and loud one time on his lab counter and glared at the boys. I understood perfectly what he was conveying without him saying a word. I DID NOT get any positive reinforcement for my correct answer.

Not long after this treatment, the teacher/coach showed up in science class with a glass gallon jar that contained a dead, yellow, and white baby anaconda (at least that's what it looked like to me). I hate snakes! The book of Genesis is true. There is enmity between me and any snake. He set the jar on top of my desk and stood beside my desk during that class period for the lesson (which had nothing to do with reptiles). The dead snake filled the jar completely! I got THAT message too. I sat with my lips feeling numb and my body literally trembling, but I never said a word or gave him the pleasure of making me cry, which I always felt was his goal. In fact, I don't think I ever answered another question aloud in that classroom again, but that didn't stop me from getting good grades on paperwork and my report card I earned while there.

There was something intimidating about that guy. I remember another evening I went with my dad to pick up William Earl after football practice. To us, it looked like all the other boys had left the fieldhouse, but we didn't see him. I wanted Daddy to go get my brother, but he would not get out of the car. After a while, that same teacher/ coach who put the snake-filled jar on my desk exited the fieldhouse. I noticed how Daddy finally rolled down his truck window, spoke softly and slowly to him, and asked if his son, McHenry, was still inside. Daddy's words were spoken with absolutely no threat in his voice. The teacher/coach spoke roughly saying he's coming out soon. I was grateful when William Earl finally emerged from the building. I never questioned daddy's behavior, but after learning history, I understood later what I didn't understand then.

It was less than fifteen years since the murder of Emmit Till in Mississippi and the protests of the Little Rock Nine students entering Central High in Arkansas. The struggle for civil rights was continuing. Here we were attending a previously all white school, and he did not want to put his child in danger because of this man's lack of good character. [4]

Band was another story. I loved being in the band at Lafayette. There, I played the clarinet, and William Earl played the tuba. At Fairview, William played football, and I never sat with the band in the band room. The band director put me in a "Practice Room." He would give me some sheet music to practice on with no other instruction or direction. Eventually, he just stopped coming by to check on me at class time, as I recall. So, I used the time as an extra study period! It didn't take a genius to see I was never going to be in his band. I cannot explain why I kept these incidents to myself for years and never told my parents. I think God shielded my mind from allowing them to get to me. God still does that even today. I seem to have what I call, "Selective Memory." To me, that's like leaving out parts of history that are hurtful or that put me in a tense state of mind. That appears to be the focus of politicians who are attempting to erase black history in America. The trouble comes when life lessons aren't learned from history and people blame others for their circumstances and fail to have compassion for anyone not of their race thinking their cultural heritage makes them better than others.

The teachers at Fairview during those days varied in their attitudes toward us. Some, I could tell immediately, wanted no part in integration. Others did their best to help us feel welcome. My favorite class was typing. Unlike at Lafayette (two or three typewriters for the whole typing class), each student at Fairview had their own typewriter in class! I excelled in that class. Mrs. Hatch even chose me to type on one of the three new electric typewriters that the school had received! She was one of my favorite teachers at Fairview. My least favorite subjects were algebra I and algebra 2 (math and I just don't get along), and band because I was not included. How I ended up with a "C" in that algebra 1 class is beyond me. I always thought I could learn anything if I had the right teacher. Well, not so in algebra.   I struggled.

It was a pleasant relief in the afternoons after school to get off the Fairview bus and board the bus from Lafayette home. There I could see the familiar faces I'd grown up with: Mr. Yarbrough and my cousins. I did, however, have an unpleasant incident on the bus one afternoon that was all my fault. My cousin started talking to me right after I had boarded the Lafayette bus. Usually, we talked about things that were funny. I didn't want to admit that I couldn't hear her above the other voices on the bus that day, so I just let out a little laugh and smiled. I could tell she was offended. She said, "I don't think that's funny." When I listened more closely, I discovered she had told me that the mother of one of my former classmates had died. I apologized and said

34

I didn't understand what she had said. It was too late. My cousin's mother had died a few years earlier, and that was why she had to move and enter school at Lafayette. For me to have laughed was an insult to her, and even though it was not intended, I still hurt her feelings. Lesson learned:

LISTEN MORE CAREFULLY; THINK BEFORE YOU SPEAK.

6. DARK DAYS

Well, life kept moving along. The Viet Nam War (referred to as a *Conflict*), the Civil Rights Movement, and the Presidential candidates were in the news. The blatant racist incidents, attempts to humiliate us (Negros) at school, and loneliness continued, but knowing the love of Jesus and my family kept my head up. That is, until I ended up in algebra 2 the following year. I was barely getting by when I got the news my brother, Carthell, had been killed in Viet Nam.

We were in the classroom of my least favorite teacher of all time. Her daily dose of meanness was not limited to ethnicity. She seemed satisfied only when she could embarrass or tease a student in class. For example, our dress code in those days did not allow girls to wear pants. I watched as this teacher called a girl up to her desk one day, and in front of the whole class, she lifted the flap of the girl's "skort," a one-piece combination of a skirt and shorts set. The girl was sent out of the classroom and home. I was embarrassed for her.

I never had any problems in any English classroom with the subject matter, but I did have a problem with this woman. I remember a class discussion about the Viet Nam conflict when she very callously said that when our soldiers get killed, they just throw their bodies into big trash bags to be shipped out.

While in her classroom, on January 26, 1968, not long after Christmas and New Year's break, beginning of Spring semester of my sophomore year, the secretary walked in and asked for me to come to the office with my things. I was clueless to the reason. I gathered my things and walked with her to the office. There I saw William Earl, Gary, and a woman from our church we called "Con" (cousin) Lillian Jean all with sad faces. Knowing something was very wrong, my panicky voice asked her, "Is it Mama?" "Was there a fire?" Lillian Jean had a speech impediment, but I understood when she said, "Cottell" with tears running down her face. I froze. Our brother, Carthell... I couldn't cry. I was numb. We walked to her car, I got in the front seat and stared at the sky like a robot. My brothers sobbed in the back seat. All my life, I have had a period of hesitation after receiving shocking news. This was my first experience of delayed emotions.

Earlier that day at lunch, I remember staring through the cafeteria's windows. The sky had looked strange to me. Had that been a premonition? I did not know. I had written my last letter to Carthell after Christmas break in early January, in the library at school. I had told him in the letter about Otis Redding's death on December 10, 1967. Carthell's last birthday was December 30, 1967. We had just received the Noritake Chinaware he had sent mama. All led to this. My big brother had been killed in Viet Nam, and his body had been "thrown into a big trash bag." Those were the thoughts in my head on Friday, January 26, 1968, the day we got the news.

As I later discovered, Mama had been at a women's meeting with the other ladies from Good Home. Their session had just ended. When exiting the church building, the ladies saw military servicemen at our house (remember, we lived right across the small dirt road from our church building). I cannot imagine the fear in my sweet, kind, gentle mother's heart as she walked toward our house. I am grateful my loving grandmothers were there, but they needed strength too. I was told that as mama walked closer to our house, one of the servicemen tried to get her to stop to talk to him, but she kept walking. God is still perfect in all HIS ways. Mama was not alone when she got the news but was surrounded by family and church family who grieved with her while making plans for informing all our family members. Long before cell phones, text messages, Facebook, etc., people got the word out as best they could. It was Lillian Jean who came for us, the three youngest children, at school. I never knew nor asked how my older siblings were told. I remember the last time he came home before leaving, Carthell assured us that everyone who goes to Viet Nam doesn't get killed... On that day, what kept running through my mind was the fact that our brother had died in Viet Nam where he had said not everyone who goes there gets killed...but he did.

Everything happening that day was surreal. When I saw the people at our house, it became reality. I was immediately sent to bed crying myself to sleep. When I woke up, I was given chicken noodle soup, the only thing my stomach could handle when I didn't feel like eating. The people kept coming for the next two weeks. The top of the big freezer in my brothers' room was covered with cakes, pies, and all sorts of non-perishable food items for our large family. Two weeks was how long it took to bring my brother's body home from Viet Nam. I learned later that my daddy and older brothers had identified Carthell's body at the funeral home when it arrived. They wanted no mistakes as there sometimes were. We would have welcomed a mistake in our case.

I was surprised to be visited by our high school principal from Fairview along with a local white pastor and his two sons. His boys were classmates of William Earl and me. They were all pleasant, but we were still trying to deal with Carthell's death. I don't remember any whites ever being in our house before that time. While the adults talked, we tried to play a game of Scrabble with the pastor's sons. The only word I could play was N -O -T. We gave up and went our separate ways, but those boys remained friendly from that time on toward our family.

Two weeks was a long time to be out of school. I tried to go back. I remember daddy driving me there after a few missed days only to turn around and bring me back home before even getting out of the car. It was too hard. Already, I was at a school where I was treated like an outsider, had that mean teacher's class to deal with, and Algebra 2 was awful even with instruction. I knew it would be terrible trying to get caught up, but my mind said I wanted to be around my family; so that was where I stayed. Family was at the forefront of my mind. Family meant love, acceptance, encouragement, and hope–things I could never get at school in 1968.

People kept visiting and bringing food. We were grateful, but the sorrow was constant. My dad did not go back to work during our wait either. I saw him break down in tears for the first time in my life when my mom's aunt and her sister who were also our neighbors, visited us to express their sympathy. When the older sister prayed, Daddy released his emotions in tears. Of course, that got us all started. That was truly our family's darkest day.

The telegram from the military came with a few details about how Carthell was killed on January 24, 1968. It said Lance Corporal James C. McHenry was leading a patrol when they came under attack. Although he and those with him took cover in a foxhole, when the firing ceased, it was his job to see if they could exit. When he raised his head, he was shot saving the lives of others with him but sacrificing his own. Carthell had turned 21 years old and only lived about a month after his birthday.

On Christmas, 1967, while on his "Rest & Recuperation" break, he had gone to Tokyo, Japan. From there he had mailed that set of Noritake China home for a Christmas gift. We got the dishes around the second week in January. Happiness turned to sorrow not long afterward with his death. That China became so special to my mom that dad had to purchase a China cabinet to display it. For years, nobody ate off those dishes. It took some coaxing from my brother, William Earl, to get mama to let him set the table for a holiday meal, and we all were very nervous but made it through without breaking anything.

Carthell's life was short, but meaningful. He had been an outstanding athlete, a smart student, an eloquent speaker, handsome, and a good singer and dancer. He made friends easily, and the ladies loved cool James Carthell McHenry. He had attended AM&N in Pine Bluff, AR, and Fresno State in California. When the nation began to draft young men into the military, Carthell, even though he was in college, said he would just go ahead and volunteer so he could choose the branch he wanted, the Marines. He liked their uniforms. Sadly, he was given the option of either staying in Washington, D.C. as an Honor Guard or going to Vietnam. Because he would have had to stay in longer as an Honor Guard, he chose Vietnam. He left behind his beloved fiancé, Gladystine Thompson, who none of us met until his funeral. I recall someone said he was asked who she looked like. He told them she looked like Wondrous. That made me feel special.

My daddy took William Earl and me with him to pick up his suit from the dry cleaners in preparing for Carthell's funeral. Daddy left us in the truck while he went inside the business. He looked disturbed when he got back in the truck. "That man just called me, 'boy.' My boy just died for the likes of that," my daddy's exact words. He was a Christian, and he didn't use profanity after the last "that." Looking back now, I wish Carthell had gone to Canada like many of the more affluent white boys who dodged the draft. He was brave and believed he owed his country his service even though it cost his life. Many talk about the Golden Rule, but African Americans and other minorities have never been given the respect, acceptance, or opportunities that many Caucasians take for granted. I think it is still called, "A sense of entitlement" that racists among us hold.

The funeral was on February 10, 1968. The weather was beautiful, and I had never seen the church so full. It was a closed casket service, and a serviceman stood beside the coffin the entire service. We could see he was sweating profusely, but he didn't move. His discipline was amazing. He honored Carthell's life. At the cemetery, I saw a military burial. The USA flag that draped the coffin was carefully removed by military attendants who folded it into a large triangle. A serviceman then presented it to my mother with the words, "From a grateful nation." I'll admit, I mumbled under my breath, "grateful nation." My thought was that my brother is dead, and there is still so much hatred in this "Grateful nation." I have never liked feeling bitter, but bitter was how I felt. Next came the twenty-one-gun salute and the playing of Taps... That was hard then and remembering now brings back the sadness.

For many years, I could not watch a war movie. I would have to leave the room and focus on anything but war. Even the battle scenes in the movie, Forest Gump, were troubling for me. I still don't watch war movies by choice. But today, when I see a veteran wearing a cap that says Viet Nam, I thank him for his service and tell him about my brother, Lance Corporal James C. McHenry.

7. MORE DARKNESS

I thought my tenth-grade year in high school had been hard enough, yet things didn't get any better.

On April 4, 1968, I was at choir practice at my church when someone walked in and announced that Dr. Martin Luther King, Jr. had been assassinated in Memphis, Tennessee. As I recall, we adjourned, and everyone went home to follow the news. What was feared had actually happened.

There was that feeling again. The sadness for the man, his wife, his children, his efforts, black people (as we were starting to be called), all minorities, and especially our country at Dr. King's death. A thirty-nine-year-old man who had used the weapon of non-violence to teach love and respect toward one another had been gunned down by a coward hiding outside the hotel where he was staying. Days of news reports and accounts of the reactions from both violent and peaceful people followed. Equality develops slowly in a racist society, but we kept holding on to his dream then and now. Like with JFK, pictures of Dr. King were displayed in homes and on church fans lest we forget to share his legacy. I can honestly say that most of what I learned about this great man came after he was gone. In life, many misunderstood him. But today, I thank God for sending Dr. Martin Luther King, Jr. He didn't get where we are now, but we would not have gotten here without his work. He was truly a blessing from God.

I remember how protective my "Brother from another mother" became of me after all the losses that school year. He was sitting beside me in the auditorium where our classes had gathered for a program. I was once again called to the office. I think my friend got as nervous as I did. He patted my head before I got up to go as if to say, "I hope everything is all right." Thank God all was well that time.

Finally, school was out for the Summer, but there was yet one more high-profile assassination, Senator Robert (Bobby) Francis Kennedy. He was campaigning for the Presidency in California when he was gunned down. I liked him, too. He left behind his wife and a lot of children. He was the younger brother of President John Fitzgerald Kennedy, who had been assassinated in 1963. He had even served in his brother's cabinet as Attorney General. Although the sadness was now very familiar, no one in their right mind wants to get used to sorrow. I heard a song on the radio in 1968, *Abraham, Martin, and John*, a fitting anthem for the times. If I didn't know that God is sovereign, I would be most miserable.

8. LIFE CONTINUES

William (as he preferred to be called) had graduated high school in the Spring of 1968 and had enrolled for the Fall semester at Southern State College in Magnolia, Arkansas. I had never heard of that school. My older siblings had attended AM&N (now UAPB) and Philander Smith in Little Rock, what are now called, "Historically Black Colleges and Universities. (HBCU)" Carthell had gone to California and attended Fresno State and AM&N before his death.

During the Spring semester of his freshman year, William needed a ride home to pick up some things for school. He got his friend, Larry Roach, from Huttig, Arkansas, to bring him home in his car along with another friend from El Dorado, Arkansas. Two college men in my front yard! One was tall, dark, handsome, and well-dressed. I was attracted to him. Larry was "flooding" (wearing pants that were too short), moccasin like sandals on his feet, and he had ashy ankles. He and I hardly even acknowledged each other. William had introduced him as "a preacher." My response was, "Are you really a preacher?" My first words to him did not get much of a response.

Larry sat on the front porch talking with my parents the whole time while the other young man tossed a baseball back and forth with my younger brother, Gary. I was wearing a green & white checkered shift dress my mama had made. I'll admit I kept trying, but he didn't seem to notice me either. Oh well.

It was my junior year in high school, and things were much better for me. The teachers were nicer. More students were acting friendlier, and I really enjoyed the classes I was taking. I even worked in the school library as an aide. By now, I had a steady boyfriend, too! That had a lot to do with my changed attitude. He was a pleasant distraction from the national news and those remaining mean-spirited students at Fairview. I was not allowed to go out on dates, but my parents did let me "Take company" when I turned sixteen. My boyfriend would catch a ride to and from my house only on Sunday afternoons. Most of the time he hitchhiked. He would start out walking and thumb his way to my house near Louann from his house in Camden, around twelve to fifteen miles. The effort he made to see me made me feel special.

On one of those Sunday visits, my little niece got a newspaper and sat in a corner chair in the dining room where she could see us sitting on the couch in the living room. She crossed her legs and held the paper up like a grownup as if we didn't see her. My parents were really watching out for me, but I think this was her idea.

Daddy put a small television in the living room where we sat, and we'd watch, talk, or look in magazines (and kiss) until Bonanza came on. That was his signal that it was time for him to leave. Of course, he had to leave by sundown, daddy's rule.

My boyfriend would call me from a pay phone every day. During the week, my younger brother, little niece, or little nephew would hide under the bed or stand nearby to listen to my side of our phone conversations. Where we lived, we had a "party line." That meant that others could pick up their phone and hear your conversation. In an emergency, you could interrupt a call and ask to use the line. My great aunt did that to me once saying she had an emergency while I was talking to my boyfriend. We ended our call. After a little, I picked up the receiver to hear her call; it was NOT an emergency. Oh well. Those were innocent days and fun.

I recall going to a football game at Lincoln High School with my daddy. I sat on the home team's side with him and my brother, Alvernon and his wife. My boyfriend joined us, and we sat behind them. I was there to babysit my nephew after the game at my brother's house.

Well, my boyfriend and I decided we wanted to walk over to the other team's side, not really caring about the game. I asked my dad, and he said "Yes" without even looking at me. Well, when the game was over, we came back to my group, and daddy was angry. He told me I was going to get a whooping because I didn't have his permission to sit somewhere else. Turns out he thought I had asked to go to the concession stand and was looking for us to come back sooner. I tried to explain that I had asked his permission, but at that moment, he was not in the mood for me to argue my case.

By the time I got home the next day, daddy had calmed down. WHEW! I had had a sleepless night worrying about coming home the next morning to a whooping. Daddy was the one who learned a life lesson that time. Lesson learned:

MAKE SURE YOU LISTEN WELL TO YOUR CHILDREN.

The one mistake my boyfriend made was bringing me gifts from time to time for no apparent reason. There was an Identification bracelet with both our names engraved on it, a wristwatch, a necklace watch, and my favorite — a big pink stuffed bunny at Easter. My mother told me to stop accepting his gifts. I realized why later in life. Some guys want to make their girlfriend think that she owes him something in return.

He started showing up at my lunchtime break at Fairview. He knew the exact time and place I would be and out of the view of any teachers. I guess he would go back to school himself, but I don't remember.

The last gift he tried to give me was a box of chocolates. I told him I couldn't accept them. He seemed hurt, and I guess he was because the next morning we saw the candy box on the ground near our house. My mother said, "Wow, I would have kept the chocolates." Lesson learned:

FOOD GIFTED TO BE SHARED WITH OTHERS IS ACCEPTABLE.

9. LOOKING TO THE FUTURE

That year at Fairview, I also became a member of the National Honor Society. There was a special assembly held and the new members had to read some information given to us by the teacher/ sponsor. There was no rehearsal nor preparation for being on stage in front of the ninth through twelfth grade students. The auditorium was full!

Today, I would have been okay, but in Spring of 1969, NOT! It seemed I had the longest part to read, and my nerves got the better of me. My voice trembled, and I couldn't control it. What was I doing in front of all these white people! Nervous beyond belief! One mean-spirited classmate referred to this occasion with a snide remark at our forty-fifth-class reunion dinner. I ignored his continued ignorance. You live and learn.

I prayed before getting on stage not long after, when I became a member of the BETA CLUB. I had to read in front of a large audience again. This time, my voice didn't tremble, and I had much more confidence. Since those days, I have never had a problem reading or speaking to a crowd.

GOD ANSWERED MY PRAYER! THANK YOU, LORD!

I was also accepted as a member of the Glee Club. I remember the tryouts involved singing a short portion of a song for the director. The white girls had to sing "Dixie" and the black girls had to sing, "Row, Row, Row Your Boat." Go figure!

One day I walked in practice and all the chairs were filled. By that time, I thought I was a little more comfortable in speaking up for myself. Looking around, I asked, "Where can I sit?" One white girl immediately blurted out," *On the floor where all n-word (plural) sit.*" I didn't respond, but she turned red, cried, and apologized freely in front of everyone. I didn't mistreat her then nor ever.

THANK YOU, LORD, FOR YOUR GIFT OF TEMPERANCE.

My senior year in high school was 1969-1970. By then, I had another boyfriend, briefly. The first one kept getting in trouble at school, and my older, wiser siblings let me know they did not approve of our relationship. The new boyfriend had come to a church service one night, and after service, he walked me home (just across the road). He visited me a couple of times, but for some reason, we just did not click. He had served his purpose. There was no bitterness or formal goodbye. Oh well!

I had plenty to keep me busy with schoolwork and preparations for graduation. I did not have a circle to travel in because my daddy would not permit me to go walking, riding, or attend social events with my cousins, classmates, or friends. Still, I looked forward to graduation and going to the same college William attended, Southern State College in Magnolia. A whole new world for me!

I did get to attend the Junior-Senior Banquet and one other event that must have meant very little to me because all I have is a picture of what I was wearing, my sister-in-law's formal gown, to say I was there. There were a few honors: "Honorable Mention" for a painting I had done, I was ranked number eleven in the "Top Twenty" of our class, and I received the "Ethel Hart Scholarship" for college. As I said earlier, my last peach tree switch encounter was at age 17, but I thank God for the disciplined life it encouraged in me"

I think it was my senior year that a group called "Up with People" visited our school and gave an outstanding performance at night. Some of the lyrics to their songs I learned have stayed with me all through life:

Up, up with people
You can see them wherever you go.
Up, up with people
They're the best kind of folks you know.
If more people were for people
All people everywhere,
There'd be a lot less people to worry about
And a lot more people who care.

Another song's lyrics I remember asked:

What color is God's skin?
What color is God's skin?
I say its black, brown, yellow,
It is red- It is white.
Every man's the same in the good Lord's sight.

People seemed to really try to get along after the previous years of darkness. Dr. King said it best, "Darkness cannot put out darkness; only light can do that. Hate cannot drive out hate; only love can do that." Lesson that needs to be learned:

THE GOLDEN RULE

Our class song was *The Age of Aquarius*, by the Fifth Dimension. I did not know how fitting that was until now. I looked forward to a better world, and I began to experience it after my high school graduation. In fact, some of the happiest days of my life were about to begin. Another opportunity with enrollment at Southern State College in Magnolia, meeting those who would become my future golden friends, and a new relationship! The young man I had met when I was in tenth grade was now a junior in college, Larry Roach! The same one with the ashy ankles! He saw me on campus and asked me to eat a meal in the cafeteria with him. And the rest is history. We ate most of our meals together the two years before he graduated, and we celebrated our 50th wedding anniversary in 2024!

There is a whole lot more that I could share, but that would require another book. The whirlwind of our college years, the ups and downs of marriage, careers, children…Whew! I think I'll ponder those memories in my heart. God always has the best life plan, and HIS grace and mercy has endured. Lesson Learned:

TRUST GOD TO ORDER YOUR STEPS IN LIFE.

10. SIBLING EXTRAS

HL: Really smart, athletic, eloquent, and handsome! Got a whooping for something, walked outside afterward and rolled his eyes at the house. He didn't know Daddy saw him. He got called back inside for another whooping. He bought my outfit for our senior class trip to Six Flags over Texas!

HL & Alvernon: Devised a plan to make daddy laugh to avoid a whooping. Alvernon was to sing to make Daddy laugh, but he started crying instead. HL kept saying, "Sing, boy, sing!" They both got their whooping.

Alvernon: I didn't know his given name for years. We called him, "Brother." His nickname for me was, "Ugly"and that kept me humble. He was Intelligent, handsome, loved math! Could jump off our front porch and run up the tree nearby. Chose my classes for me at Fairview – Algebra 1 & 2, UGH!!!

Melvia: I didn't know her given name for years either. We called her, "Sister." Beautiful and spoke her mind. Multi-talented: crafts, sewing, stylist, etc. She made yellow and white checkered dresses for herself, Geneva, and me. She called me her "Baby doll."

Geneva: Beautiful diva! Friendly, stylish, never met a stranger. Knows how to enjoy her life and be her unique self. True California girl! She knows how to encourage the best in people. Afraid of live chickens after being chased by Jessie with one as a child.

Jessie: My cool brother. So smart he was double promoted causing him to graduate from high school much younger than his classmates. Handsome and very intuitive. Lady magnet!

Carthell: Jessie taught him to be cool. He was athletic, smart, handsome, could sing, and loved by the ladies wherever he went. He was called "Mac" and made a lot of friends. He cried when he hit a tree in our yard while showing off his driving skill (or lack thereof). Gone too soon…

William: Pretended to go blind to avoid getting a whooping. Tried a hairstyle that I had to assist him with so his scalp would stop burning! Carthell taught him to be cool. Well-liked, handsome, and more agreeable as he grew up. He set his goals and exceeded them. Intelligent but couldn't spell!

Gary: William taught him to be cool. Had little tolerance for kittens that jumped off his little red wagon. Survived being struck by lightning that traveled through phone lines! Smart, athletic, handsome, and enjoyed all the benefits of being the youngest – few or no switches!

LANGUAGE

Daddy's favorite words when he was upset: *"I be John Brown!"*

Mama's favorite phrase when she was upset: *"Sh___, uh oh!"*

My favorite word when I was upset: *"Shoot!"*

11. STORY NOTES

1. Whipping/whooping-- spanking/thrashing-- only with a peach tree switch in our house/ No belts, extension cords, shoes, brushes, or hands as some parents used. I could have called it a whipping , but whooping is more accurate to me, because of the sound made by the one being punished.

2. African American - Our race was referred to as Colored, Negro, Black, and another term I will not dignify, but you can guess in the late 50's— late 60's.

3. French port - a small community on Camden's mail and school bus routes.

4. There was a twist to my encounters with this teacher- coach. In the mid 80's, I saw him. I was married, had three children, and was a fifth grade teacher. I had seen his name on a sign outside a small house/office in another town about forty-five minutes from our home. I told my children that if a car was there when we headed home, we would stop. There was, and we did. Walking through the front door, I saw him sitting behind a desk. I asked, "Do you remember me?" He responded, "Wondrous McHenry," stood up from his desk, walked up, and hugged me. He asked about my parents and my family. I returned the hug, introduced my children, and we conversed briefly. Neither of us mentioned the snake incident nor anything else about those days.

Maya Angelou is quoted for saying, *"You may not control all the events that happen to you, but you can decide not to be reduced by them."*

THANK GOD FOR FORGIVING US AS WE FORGIVE OTHERS!

About the Author

Wondrous Marie McHenry-Roach graduated from Fairview High School in Camden, Arkansas, and Southern State College (now Southern Arkansas University) in Magnolia, Arkansas. She is a retired educator from the Magnolia Public School system, where she taught fifth grade for many years. Wondrous and her husband, Larry Wayne Roach, have three children, eight grandchildren, and two great-grandsons. Together, they lead Greater Harvest Church of God in Christ, a church Larry founded and has pastored since 1983 in Magnolia, Arkansas. Their ministry has nurtured many spiritual sons and daughters over the years.